HOW TO PLAN AND INVEST FOR YOUR RETIREMENT

This No Nonsense Guide shows you what to expect from Social Security and company pension plans and what you need to know about:
- IRAs
- 401 (K)s
- Money Market Accounts
- Asset allocation
- Other sources of income

THE NO NONSENSE LIBRARY
NO NONSENSE FINANCIAL GUIDES:

How to Choose a Discount Stockbroker, Revised Edition
How to Finance Your Child's College Education, Revised Edition
How to Plan and Invest for Your Retirement
How to Use Credit and Credit Cards, Revised Edition
The New Tax Law and What It Means to You
Personal Banking
Understanding Common Stocks, Revised Edition
Understanding Insurance
Understanding IRAs, Revised Edition
Understanding Money Market Funds, Revised Edition
Understanding Mutual Funds, Revised Edition
Understanding Social Security
Understanding the Stock Market, Revised Edition
Understanding Stock Options and Futures Markets, Revised Edition
Understanding Tax-Exempt Bonds
Understanding Treasury Bills and Other U.S. Government Securities,
  Revised Edition

OTHER NO NONSENSE GUIDES:

Car Guides
Career Guides
Cooking Guides
Health Guides
Legal Guides
Parenting Guides
Photography Guides
Real Estate Guides
Study Guides
Success Guides
Wine Guides

NO NONSENSE FINANCIAL GUIDE®

HOW TO PLAN AND INVEST FOR YOUR RETIREMENT

Irene Blankson
Kevin Powell

Longmeadow Press

This publication is designed to provide accurate and authoritative information with regard to the subject matter covered. It is sold with the understanding that neither the publisher nor the authors are engaged in rendering legal, accounting, or other professional service regarding the subject matter covered. If legal advice or other expert assistance is desired, the services of a competent professional should be sought.

HOW TO PLAN AND INVEST FOR YOUR RETIREMENT

Copyright © 1991 by Longmeadow Press

No Nonsense Financial Guide is a trademark controlled by Longmeadow Press.

Published by Longmeadow Press, 201 High Ridge Road, Stamford, Connecticut 06904. No part of this book may be reproduced or used in any form or by any means, electronic or mechanical, including photocopying, recording, or by an information storage and retrieval system, without permission in writing from the publisher.

ISBN 0-681-41048-5

Production services: Marie Brown Associates
Cover and inside design: Ken Brown
Editing/copyediting: Karen Taylor
Typography: ANY Phototype, Inc.

Printed in the United States of America

0   9   8   7   6   5   4   3   2   1

CONTENTS

Chapter 1	Making Retirement A Comfort	1
Chapter 2	What To Expect From Social Security	5
Chapter 3	What To Expect From Company Pension Plans	13
Chapter 4	IRAs: What You Need To Know	19
Chapter 5	401 (K)s: What You Need To Know	23
Chapter 6	Mutual Funds	27
Chapter 7	Keoghs: Savings For The Self-Employed	31
Chapter 8	Asset Allocation And Some Basic Truths About Investing	35
Chapter 9	Medicare And You	39
Chapter 10	The Estimated Tax Syndrome	43
Chapter 11	Early Retirement Possibilities	47
	Glossary	67
	Index	75

AMERICAN ASSOCIATION FOR RETIRED PERSONS

This is a non-profit, non-partisan organization that is dedicated to helping retired Americans achieve lives of independence, dignity, and purpose. Membership is available to anyone aged 50 or older, regardless of their employment status.

For information about association activities or for answers to questions you may have about life after retirement, contact your local office or call national headquarters in Washington, D.C. at (202) 728-4780.

1

MAKING RETIREMENT
A COMFORT

In today's society, retirement involves a number of factors which were not evident two or three decades ago. For instance, the average American now lives 10 to 20 years beyond his or her retirement age. Even that statistic is tricky. Given the advances of medical technology, many Americans will be living to and beyond the age of 90—nearly a third of our lives could be spent in retirement.

Consequently, you can look to retirement as much more than restless inactivity with little financial recourse for sustenance. Unfortunately, many retirees find that the regularity of payments from their former employers and the Social Security Administration leave a bit to be desired. And if your career allowed you to become self-employed, you may face the additional obstacle of mapping out your own savings plan. Given the ever-present realities of inflation, income received from these programs may not even cover your basic living expenses. After working hard for many years, you deserve much more than these traditional options are usually able to give.

2 MAKING RETIREMENT A COMFORT

Emphasis today should be on IRAs, KEOGHS, and money market accounts. Designed specifically for long-term investment, these types of accounts can reap healthy benefits from careful planning now. Research the savings plans and incentives offered by institutions before making a choice. For instance, Individual Retirement Accounts (IRAs) can be set up at one financial institution or many; just be careful when you open multiple accounts because most institutions charge annual fees which can run up to and above $50 to maintain the account.

If you are self-employed, a KEOGH plan is ideal. The name comes from the late New York Congressman Eugene Keogh, architect of the 1962 Self-Employed Individuals Retirement Act. Congress allowed the self-employed to have the same opportunity to save for retirement as those who were employed by someone else. Hence, the monies you put away in a KEOGH are deductible on your Federal income tax return. One other advantage of such a plan is that the money in the plan builds up tax-deferred until it's withdrawn. We'll investigate this avenue further in Chapter 7.

Money market accounts can be thought of as limited checking accounts, in the sense that you can only write a few checks per month. These accounts pay interest but usually in some relation to market rates. The best part of a money market account is that you can pull your cash out immediately, and at any time. Also, your principal and interest—up to $100,000 are protected by the Federal government as long as the bank is a member of the FDIC.

In addition, you, the wise retiree, should watch Congress for tax revenue increases that may affect retirement planning. How comfortably you spend your retirement years is directly dependent on the strategies you employ well before retirement. The adage "failing to prepare is preparing to fail" is apropos.

The first step in planning is to decide what it is you will want during retirement and then estimate the amount

MAKING RETIREMENT A COMFORT 3

of capital required. The best way to calculate what you need after retirement is to review your present expenditures. Obviously, you will at least want to maintain your current standard of living. Again, your financial planning should take inflation into account. Do you own a car? A house? Are there any outstanding debts? Do you have any dependents?

With more time on your hands, you may also want to do some things not possible earlier in life, such as travel or continue your education. Just because you're no longer working at a 9-to-5, you need not feel limited—instead of a two-week vacation, you can take two months!

Sound retirement financial planning is not something that you do once—it's perpetual.

How an "Average" Older (65+) Urban Household Spends Its Money:

Housing:	33 %
Food:	16.1%
Transportation:	15.4%
Medical Care:	10.2%
Clothing and personal care:	6.7%
Contributions:	5 %
Entertainment, Education, Reading:	5 %
Other Expenses:	7.9%

Source: U.S. Bureau of Labour Statistics, 1987

2

WHAT TO EXPECT FROM SOCIAL SECURITY

In order to understand what you can expect from Social Security, you must first learn its history.

The 1935 Social Security Act was created to provide retirement benefits for employed Americans. Of course, much has changed since then, but Social Security basically provides four types of benefits:

- Retirement benefits for workers, spouses, and dependent children of retirees. These benefits currently begin at age 65, or at a reduced level at age 62;

- Survivor's benefits for the spouse, minor children, and dependent elderly parents of a worker who dies;

- Disability benefits for a worker who is unable to work for an extended period. Benefits are also paid to the spouse and children of a disabled worker; and

6 WHAT TO EXPECT FROM SOCIAL SECURITY

- Medical insurance (Medicare), beginning at the age of 65, and for disabled workers who have been receiving disability payments for at least 24 months.

QUALIFYING
FOR
BENEFITS

You must work for a specific period of time in covered employment to obtain insured status. In the official language of the Social Security Administration, you may receive total benefits if you are "fully insured." How do you know if you're fully insured? Read on and see.

The government requires a certain amount of calendar quarters of coverage from each worker—40, to be exact—to guarantee benefits. A calendar quarter is credited to your records for every $520 you earn during a year up to the maximum of four quarters every year. So, if you've been doing your math, you'll have calculated that a total of ten years of work will do the trick. After this time, you're insured for life, even if you choose to never work again.

With fully insured status, you and your family may receive retirement and disability benefits, and your family also receives protection in case of your death. Retirement benefits are payable to the following:

- The insured worker, aged 62 or over.
- Spouse or divorced spouse, aged 62 or over.
- Spouse, any age, if caring for a child under age 18.
- Children or grandchildren (if qualified as above).

The Social Security Administration also has a provision for you if you have worked for less than ten years called "currently insured" status. Even if you have fewer than ten years in covered employment you may still be eligible under one of the many qualifying scenarios outlined by the Administration.

WHAT TO EXPECT FROM SOCIAL SECURITY 7

Currently insured status is designed to help families of those who die without having enough coverage to qualify for retirement benefits. If you are currently insured at the time you die, survivor benefits are payable to:

- Your unmarried children (or dependent grandchildren whose parents are dead or disabled) if under 18 or disabled regardless of their ages.
- Your spouse (or divorced spouse), if caring for your child if under 18.

Also payable under the currently insured status are lump-sum death benefits to a spouse or eligible child.

The more money your earn, the more you can expect in benefits during retirement. You should confirm your earnings history with the Social Security Administration every three years or so. Doing this will enable you to accurately tabulate your retirement earnings.

In your retirement planning, it does not pay to put all your eggs in one basket. Working spouses should note that they have their own earnings record and they can collect benefits on their own. One spouse need not wait until the other spouse retires in order to collect benefits. Working spouses receive the higher of the worker's benefit or the spousal benefit, but not both.

A divorced spouse may collect on the account of his or her former retired spouse (the insured worker) if the marriage lasted ten years or longer before ending in divorce.

If the insured worker remarries, the former non-working spouse may collect on his or her account, even if the insured's new spouse is also collecting. But if the non-working, divorced spouse remarries, he or she may not collect on the former spouse's account. The remarried spouse can collect only on the account of the new spouse.

However, if the second marriage ends in divorce after ten years, he or she may collect on the account of either former spouse. If the second marriage ends in divorce in less than ten years, he or she may collect only on the

8 WHAT TO EXPECT FROM SOCIAL SECURITY

account of the first spouse. But if the insured spouse of the second marriage dies after one year, the uninsured spouse may collect on the account of the deceased.

A divorced person who takes care of a former spouse's children is eligible for benefits when the former spouse dies or retires, even if the marriage did not last ten years. Children of a divorced couple are eligible for dependent's or survivor's benefits on the record of either parent. Their benefits are not affected by the custody or support arrangement of their divorced parents.

Benefits to a widow or widower usually end if she or he remarries. However, this rule does not apply if the widow or widower is aged 60 or older when the second marriage takes place. An individual may receive a benefit on the account of the new spouse if it would be larger than the widow's or widower's benefit.

KNOW
YOUR
SHARE

There is a ceiling on the amount of benefits that may be paid to you on your account. Since 1979, the Social Security Administration has used a method called wage indexing to compute the amount of benefits to pay each worker. Your benefits are based on the "indexed" earnings over a fixed period of years after 1950.

The only wages used will be the ones credited to your Social Security account.

Note in the following table the maximum amount of wages that Social Security will tax for particular years.

WHAT TO EXPECT FROM SOCIAL SECURITY

YEAR	EARNINGS
1990	$51,300
1989	48,000
1988	45,000
1987	43,800
1986	42,000
1985	39,600
1984	37,800
1983	35,700
1982	32,400
1981	29,700
1980	25,900
1979	22,900
1978	17,700
1977	16,500
1976	15,300
1975	14,100
1974	13,200
1973	10,800
1972	9,000
1968-1971	7,800
1966-1967	6,600
1959-1965	4,800
1955-1958	4,200
1951-1954	3,600

10 WHAT TO EXPECT FROM SOCIAL SECURITY

TRACKING
YOUR
EARNINGS

You should keep a record of your earnings and payment of Social Security taxes (FICA) and compare it to the record of the Office of Central Operations of the Social Security Administration. Ask your Social Security office for form SSA-7004-PC, or the "Request for Earnings and Benefit Estimate Statement." You can also obtain a copy of the form from your local post office.

Once you have completed the form, you should mail it to: Social Security Administration, Wilkes-Barre Data Operations Center, P.O. Box 20, Wilkes-Barre, PA 18711. The Social Security Administration will send you a statement of your covered earnings and include an estimate of your future benefits based on an income projection you provide on the form.

You should receive a response within six weeks. If the Social Security Administration statement contains errors regarding your earnings, you should contact the office immediately to make corrections.

TAKE
NOTE

You may be taxed on up to 50 percent of your benefits if your income exceeds a particular amount. The amount of your benefits plus your other income will determine whether your benefits are taxable or not.

There is a simple two-step process to figure out the taxation of your benefits. First, you must determine

WHAT TO EXPECT FROM SOCIAL SECURITY   11

whether your income exceeds a base amount for your filing status. Once you have this amount, calculate the amount of your benefits subject to tax.

STEP ONE

Starting with your adjusted gross income, add 50 percent of your Social Security benefits, tax-exempt interest, excluded foreign earned income, and excluded income from US possessions or Puerto Rico. If you are single and your adjusted gross income, increased by this step, exceeds $25,000, or if you are married, filing jointly and the adjustment exceeds $32,000, part of your benefits are taxable.

For the purpose of this exercise, IRA deductions are not considered in figuring adjusted gross income. If you determine that part of your benefits are taxable, then add them to your adjusted gross income to assess whether you're eligible for an IRA deduction according to the phaseout rules noted in Chapter 4.

If you find that you are allowed an IRA deduction according to the rules, then redo Step One by reducing your adjusted gross income by the allowable IRA deduction.

Now you may proceed to Step Two.

STEP TWO

The amount of your benefits that will be taxable is 50 percent of the excess over the base amount, or 50 percent of your benefits, whichever is the smaller amount.

WHAT TO EXPECT FROM SOCIAL SECURITY

Where will your retirement income come from?

Americans who hope to retire with an annual income of at least $20,000 will receive this money from the following sources:

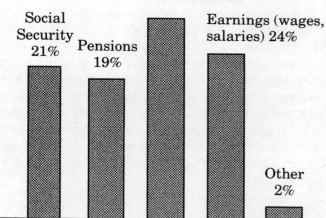

Source: Social Security Administration, 1988

3

WHAT TO EXPECT FROM COMPANY PENSION PLANS

A company pension plan can be a vital source of income one day. As an employee looking towards retirement, you should consider three important questions:
- Who contributes to the plan?
- What happens to the money in the plan?
- How do I take my money out?

In this chapter we will examine each of these questions and provide some answers and avenues for you to explore further.

QUALIFIED PLANS

The Internal Revenue Service only approves plans that have met certain standards of eligibility, benefits, and reporting. These qualified plans are then able to offer tax deductions for contributions, tax-free accumulations of income, and special tax treatment for distribution.

14 WHAT TO EXPECT FROM COMPANY PENSION PLANS

Each company has the option of several qualified plans: the pension plan, profit-sharing plan, stock-bonus plan, thrift plan, or a combination of plans.

Pension plans are designed to provide you with a fixed benefit when you retire. There are two types of pension plans—defined-benefit and defined-contribution plans.

With defined-benefit plans, your employer usually makes all the contributions. The benefits are at a fixed amount and the contributions are geared to providing those benefits when you retire. Three factors are important in determining how much you will receive from this plan: your salary, your length of service with the company, and the percentage that your plan's formula uses.

Your final average salary may be determined by your highest five years of earnings, the highest five out of ten years, your career average, or other means, depending on your plan. The percentage used is applied to the final average of your salary. In many cases, plans use two or three different percentages, which are based on Social Security earnings.

The monies earned by the plan funds may affect contributions in that, if the fund earns more than the rate determined at the plan's inception, the company may decrease its contributions. On the other hand, the IRS may request increased contributions if the fund's earnings did not reach expectations.

When a company uses defined-contribution plans, it commits to making a fixed annual contribution regardless of the profit margin. A good example is the money-purchase plan, which may require up to 10 percent of each participant's salary in contributions. In this case, contributions plus earnings on the fund determine the benefits.

Younger employees tend to favor programs such as the money-purchase plan since the number of participating years is a major factor. While you may favor the perks of the defined-benefits plan, as you approach retirement, be aware that new laws prohibit the initiation of these plans shortly before retirement age.

WHAT TO EXPECT FROM COMPANY PENSION PLANS   15

Profit-sharing plans do not have fixed benefits. The contributions are made from the company's profits and appropriated to each employee according to a specific formula. The amount remains constant regardless of whether the plan participant is a stockholder, officer, or executive. At the date of payment, the employee will receive the monies designated for his or her account plus the income and capital appreciation attributable to the allocation.

When choosing the best plan for your needs, you should examine the earnings history of your company. Pension plans will require contributions sufficient to pay you once you retire, regardless of profit. The law imposes standards on corporations to meet this obligation, and the contributions are calculated based on that.

Profit-sharing plans do not require that your company pay a fixed amount into the fund. For better or for worse, contributions are based on profits. So in loss years, you may receive nothing, while hefty gains may be made in prosperous times. Or, contributions may be made based on projected earnings; it is not written in stone that companies apportion profit-sharing funds in direct ratio to their earnings—either current or accrued. Given this scenario, employees are usually given many incentives to ensure company solvency. On the other hand, pension plans offer employee security through predetermined benefits.

Employee stock ownership plans, known as ESOPs, invest in the stock of the corporation hosting the plan. So your retirement benefit and the stock's growth depends on how well your corporation does financially.

A good thing to know about ESOPs is that when you reach the age of 55, the rules allow you to move a portion of your account into other plans. Generally, plans that invest chiefly in company stock make that option available for qualified participants.

Also important to note is that the US government also contributes to these plans, but there is a ceiling. You may receive the lesser of 25 percent of your annual earnings or

WHAT TO EXPECT FROM COMPANY PENSION PLANS

$30,000. This applies to all of your defined-contribution plans.

TAKING
YOUR MONEY
OUT

In some cases, you will have a choice to withdraw money from your retirement plan. You may be able to either remove it all at once in a lump sum, or receive it over a period of time in an annuity.

Lump sum withdrawals and annuities are designed to be "actuarially equivalent," or in English, you should receive the same amount of money no matter which method you choose. You should make your choice according to your marital status, your age and your spouse's, and your financial resources at the time of retirement.

There are several kinds of annuities available to you. One kind, single-life, distributes your annuity over the course of your life. Joint and survivor (J&S) annuities pay your benefits to you and your mate as long as either one of you live. A third type of annuity pays benefits for a particular amount of time only.

In comparing single-life to joint and survivor annuities, you should know a few facts. First, the monthly payment you will receive from a J&S plan will be less than that of a single-life, because the monies are being distributed over a potentially longer period of time—that is, two lives instead of one. Also, J&S and single-life annuity plans render the same amount of money at the time of collection. Practical thinking is also crucial in making your decision. If, for instance, you feel you will outlive your spouse, a single-life annuity may be the best option. Should you feel your spouse will outlive you, the J&S plan will most likely be the best choice for both of you.

WHAT TO EXPECT FROM COMPANY PENSION PLANS 17

If your spouse has their own pension plan, then, of course, income from your retirement plan will not be crucial to their survival. A single-life plan would be wise in this case.

If you decide to use a J&S annuity in your planning, note that you will have to select a percentage—between 50 and 100—of the annuity for your spouse to receive once you die. Laws require you to get your spouse's consent if you choose a percentage less than 50.

Now, the other method of withdrawing your money is to do it all at once, known as a lump-sum withdrawal. The government provides a few options for lump-sum withdrawals. You can either invest the funds in an Individual Retirement Account and postpone paying taxes, or pay taxes at the time of withdrawal. You can also invest 50 percent or more of the monies into an IRA, thereby delaying tax payments on that amount.

Should you decide not to invest the lump-sum, there is another avenue available by law called five-year forward averaging. This method of paying taxes may save you money because it allows you to make your payments as though you received your monies over a five-year period instead of all at once.

Be sure to note that there are some requirements that you must meet before you can use five-year averaging in your tax computations. The first thing you should know is that you may use the method only once in your life and only after you have reached the age of $59\frac{1}{2}$.

Next, you should know that you must have joined your particular retirement plan five years before withdrawing the monies. If the money is being withdrawn because of death, this stipulation is waived.

You also have to be sure to receive the total amount of the withdrawal in one calendar year. The withdrawal is payable should you become disabled, if you die, or if you or your company terminates your employment.

4

IRAs: WHAT YOU NEED TO KNOW

Individual Retirement Accounts (IRAs) may not be as lucrative as they once were but they still can be a path to a secure retirement. IRAs are, technically, trustee or custodial accounts, with either the savings establishment, brokerage firm, or mutual fund seller you do business with as the executor.

You also have the choice to play an active role in how your investments are planned with an account called the "self-directed" plan. With the bank or financial institution handling your account, you would actually make the investment decisions yourself. The fees involved for these types of programs may be high, though, so plans should be geared for the time you have developed a large account.

Much will depend on your ability to analyze your personal situation carefully and several key factors, including your age, the length of time until your retirement, and your Federal and state tax rates.

The government puts no restriction on the number of IRA accounts you may have—but you may want to. If each account bears an annual maintenance fee of $100, for

20 IRA's: WHAT YOU NEED TO KNOW

instance, that will greatly reduce your income. These maintenance fees are not tax deductible, either, unless certain conditions specified by law are met.

DEDUCTIBLES

Before your begin your investigation of IRA accounts, you should check the last W-2 statement you received for a box called "pension plan." If the box is checked, the government has evaluated your status as active, meaning that you are eligible to participate in a retirement plan.

As an active participant, you make take a full $2,000 deductible if your adjusted gross income is $25,000 or less. For every $50 you earn above $25,000, the deduction allowed drops by $10. This "phase-out" continues until you reach $35,000, at which point the deduction is $0.

If you are married, and either of you is a participant, and your adjusted gross income (AGI) is $40,000 or less, you may make a full deduction. The "phase-out" is applied as explained earlier until you reach an AGI of $50,000.

FUND TRANSFERS

There are two kinds of fund transfers you may make with your IRA dollars. The first is known as a direct trustee-to-trustee transfer. In this case, the monies never come into your possession. The institution executing your account would send the funds to another institution at which you've already initiated another account. This type of transfer can be done as many times during a year as you wish, with no governmental penalty. Note, though, that the institutions involved may decide to penalize your account with a loss of interest, for example, for this type of transaction. Another possibility is that the interest on your account may be reduced as low as the passbook rates because the bank may regard the transaction as an early withdrawal as opposed to a transfer. Check the fine print of your bank's programs before you make a move.

Roll-overs are different in that the money actually comes into your possession for a period of time, that is, when you withdraw the money from one IRA to deposit it into another. There is 60-day grace period you have to make any roll-over. After this time, the government will treat it as a withdrawal and tax you accordingly. You will also have to pay the 10 percent penalty fee imposed on early withdrawals, so move quick.

Finally, you should know that one roll-over a year is allowed where you will be permitted to pay regular income taxes on the monies, and not have to pay the 10 percent penalty on the account.

WHERE TO INVEST

Once you withdraw monies from your IRA account, one of your options is to invest again. You may invest your IRA monies in any of the areas you normally would for your retirement planning—be it a CD, mutual fund, stocks, or bonds. You should not expect to be able to purchase ancient artifacts or a life insurance policy, though. If you choose to make such an expenditure on collectibles before the age of 59½, you will also be responsible for a 10 percent penalty, so use your discretion.

Municipal bonds are definitely a 'no-no' when looking to invest your IRA dollars. The reason being is that any withdrawal from your fund will be taxed by the government. Municipal bonds are tax free, so putting money from one area to another would be creating taxes out of none.

DIPPING INTO YOUR PRINCIPAL

If you invest $10,000 at 7% interest, compounded quarterly, you can withdraw the following monthly amounts for the stated number of years, after which the $10,000 will be depleted:

Monthly Withdrawal	Length of Time
$ 116	10 years
89	15 years
77	20 years
70	25 years
59	Indefinitely; you are drawing interest only

A starting lump sum of $10,000 actually yields $21,000 if withdrawn over a 25-year period: $70 a month times 300 months equal $21,000. You can figure monthly withdrawals based on any lump sum investment. Multiply the figures above by the number of tens of thousands of dollars in the starting lump sum. For example, for $25,000, multiply the above figures by 2.5. On a 25-year withdrawal plan, the monthly withdrawal plan, the monthly withdrawal is: 2.5 times *$70* equals *$175. The withdrawal amount will differ with different interest rates.*

5

401 (K)s: WHAT YOU NEED TO KNOW

This is a tax-favorable, company-sponsored retirement savings plan that was created out of the Internal Revenue Code. There are many reasons why it would be wise to investigate a 401 (K). First, like IRAs, you pay no income taxes on the monies involved until you withdraw them—which will most likely be at retirement. Also, your interest, dividends, and other earnings will accrue tax deferred until you take the funds out. Do not make the dreadful mistake of thinking that tax-deferred funds are the same as tax-free monies. The deferment means that taxes are due upon withdrawal.

Company-sponsored plans carry the added plus of up to a 50 percent return on your investment. Many companies usually match up to 50 cents of every dollar an employee invests. However, this is usually applicable to only six percent of the entire contribution, at best. There are one of two ways you may receive contributions from your company. Your employer may make contributions of a certain amount to your trust account, on which you will not be taxed. Or, you may forego a salary increase or accept

24 401(K)s: WHAT YOU NEED TO KNOW

a salary reduction. The monies created from whichever decision you choose will be placed in a trust fund for you, and will be considered your employer's contribution.

If you choose to take a salary reduction, one of the first things you should note is that there is a maximum salary reduction that is actually a percentage of compensation. To actually enroll in the plan, all you need to do is notify your company benefits office. The company's trustees will then set up and administer the plan. Contributions are then automatic; they are held back from your pay and shifted directly to your plan.

Again, there are restrictions as to when you may withdraw the funds. You must have reached 59½, retired, become separated from the service by retirement or termination, become disabled, or show financial hardship. And as we noted with IRAs, withdrawals made before you turn 59½ are subject to the 10 percent penalty.

As an educated consumer, you should know that, by law, 401 (K) plans are not to discriminate based on levels of income. There are two ways to discern if anything is amiss. The first method is called the coverage test, and the second is the contribution test.

Under the stipulations of the coverage test, plan years starting after 1988 must meet one of the following requirements:

- Seventy percent of all low- to medium-income employees must be covered;
- The percentage of low- to medium-income employees with benefits may be 70 percent of the participating highly-paid employees; or
- An "average benefits test" is satisfied.

The contribution test, for plan years beginning after 1986, compare highly-paid employees to other eligible employees. Highly-compensated employees must have, during the current or preceding years:

401(K)S: WHAT YOU NEED TO KNOW   25

- Owned more than 5 percent of the company;
- Been officers with compensation over $45,000;
- Had compensation over $75,000;
- Had compensation over $50,000 and were in the top-paid 20 percent of all employees.

People employed by public institutions like colleges and universities may not participate in 401 (K)s according to law. A 403 (b) plan has been developed for them. They are similar to 401 (K)s in that an agreed upon sum is subtracted from your paycheck and deposited. You are not currently taxed on the account, and monies build up tax deferred until withdrawal. The government imposes a ceiling of $9,500 or 20 percent of your earnings each year, whichever is the lesser amount.

So, in the final analysis, a 401 (K) plan is a very wise choice. Tax deferment, as well as matching contributions from your employer, is nothing to sneeze at.

6

MUTUAL FUNDS

Mutual funds are very flexible varied programs that allow you to investigate each of the four areas of investment we will discuss in Chapter 8. With most institutions that handle mutual funds, you can expect your individual portfolio to be handled by an expert in the field.

Also know that, with mutual funds, you will automatically have a diversified allocation of your assets, which should be explained to you by your representative. Another plus is that withdrawals and deposits are almost as simple as doing so at a regular savings or commercial bank.

MONEY
MARKET
PLANS

Money market accounts are available at banks and savings and loan institutions, and can be considered limited checking accounts that allow you to write a few

28 MUTUAL FUNDS

checks each month that pay interest. One very favorable thing about money market accounts is that your money is always readily available with no penalty involved. Another plus is insurance by the Federal government on up to $100,000, as long as the institution you are banking with is a member of the Federal Deposit Insurance Corporation or the National Credit Union Administration.

One item to keep in mind is that money market accounts offer no guaranteed fixed interest rate. Institutions that carry the accounts aren't bound by law to tie their rates to any market indicator, and, therefore, often offer rates lower than those on CDs. So if you are already retired, you might not want to put too much money in a money market account to ensure a certain amount of income each month. A good way to gauge yourself is to keep no more than three-month's living expenses in a money market account.

In essence, money market accounts might be best used as emergency funds, but not for long-term planning.

When you are investigating money market accounts in different institutions, be sure to ask questions. After all, it is your money. What is the history of the establishment? What yield does it offer? What are the minimum balances required? Are there any charges for checks that you will write? What about other restrictions, if any?

Again, questions and decisions regarding your retirement now can have either a tremendous negative or positive impact on a major part of your life.

When looking at money market funds, know that they are not insured by a state or government agency, but they do pay a much higher rate of interest than money market accounts. A great deal of funds require a minimum deposit amount and withdrawal amount.

There are three different types of money market funds which are usually determined by the types of securities the funds are invested in. General purpose funds buy a wide variety of securities, including short-term government bills, corporate notes, and certificates of deposit.

Government funds invest in securities issued by the Federal government only, thereby offering the highest level of safety to the fund owners. Non-taxable funds invest in the Federal tax-exempt state and local obligations only. These funds pay dividends at a lower rate than the other two funds.

CERTIFICATES
OF DEPOSIT

CDs carry varying interest rates, so it would be best to investigate those offered by more than one institution before making a decision. Technically, participating in a CD is a mutually beneficial agreement between you and your banking institution. Once you place your money in the account, the bank is able to make use of the money for a prescribed amount of time, and in return, you will be paid interest based on that same time period.

When doing your CD shopping, be sure to look at the yield as well as the interest rate offered. A seemingly high rate compounded annually may not render as much income in the long run as a slightly lower rate compounded quarterly, or a much lower rate compounded daily.

A "red flag" should go up when an institution offers interest rates at a much higher percentage than the standard rate for CDs. The bank may be in need of funds or on its way out, for that matter, so be careful. Another thing to look out for is CDs with maturity periods of longer than two years. If they take that long to mature, they are more like bonds than the cash equivalent investments you are looking for.

Increased susceptibility to fluctuating interest rates and inflation is an issue to consider when looking at longer-term CDs. So check the withdrawal provisions and restrictions; at times, you may wind up paying, to the

MUTUAL FUNDS

financial institution, the entire amount of interest accrued in your account in high penalties.

Brokerage houses also see CDs, often at a higher interest rate. Of course, you'll be paying a brokerage fee. The reason for the higher rate is that the houses often purchase several CDs from banks all at once, which allows for more flexibility. Because brokers deal in the secondary market for CDs, they can sell your certificate to another investor after you have withdrawn, thereby reducing the house's need to penalize you for early withdrawal.

WHICH
IS RIGHT
FOR ME?

Dependent on what your particular situation calls for, be it safety, liquidity, saving taxes, convenience, or return, you will have to make your decision work for you.

7

KEOGHS: SAVINGS FOR THE SELF-EMPLOYED

One way to further ensure a comfortable retirement is to investigate all possible means of income. A savings account that has been accumulating steadily during your working years is a very good choice for ready income.

A Keogh plan is a wise choice for you if you are in business for yourself, for a few good reasons: tax deductions claimed for contributions can be made to the plan; accumulations of tax-free income earned on assets held by the plan; and special averaging provisions for lump-sum benefits paid on retirement.

In deciding whether to initiate a Keogh plan, there are a few factors to consider.

By law, you are required to include your employees on the plan. Such being the case, you must make contributions to each of their plans. The good thing about this arrangement is that the contributions you make are deductible. Keep in mind, though, that the more employees you have, the greater the contributions you must make; a substantial payroll might nullify the tax savings you may reap on your account.

32 KEOGHS: SAVINGS FOR THE SELF-EMPLOYMENT

Consider your expendable available income. After your personal and business expenses are met, do you have cash you can feasibly contribute to the fund?

Next, as is the case with IRAs, you will be penalized on any withdrawals made before the age of 59½. Be sure to keep other emergency funds available so you don't have to resort to your Keogh in times or urgency.

You are eligible to start a Keogh if you are earning income from the performance of personal services. According to the specifications of Keoghs, earned income is your net profit (*i.e.*, gross business or professional income less allowable business deductions). These earnings may be from your main occupation or from a sideline business.

If you are a limited partner or retired partner still receiving monies from the partnership, you cannot make contributions to the Keogh plan.

MAKING A CHOICE

You should know that there are two kinds of Keogh plans. One is called the defined-benefit plan and the other is called the defined-contribution plan. Defined-benefit plans allow you to provide for, in advance, a particular retirement benefit based on contributions made, derived from an IRS formula and risk estimations.

In terms of your limitations, the maximum annual retirement benefit may not exceed $94,023. Your maximum contribution will be an amount determined to provide that benefit when you retire.

Retirement benefits under defined-contribution plans depend on the contributions made to your account and your employees' account over the time period the plan is active. If contributions are geared towards profit, the plan is a profit-sharing plan; if not, the plan is a money-purchase pension plan. If you opt for the latter, you must contribute

KEOGHS: SAVINGS FOR THE SELF-EMPLOYMENT

to their accounts even if you have no earnings and aren't permitted to contribute to your own account.

If contributions are based on profits, allocations to your account and to your employees' account can only be made in years of profit. Recognize that the limitations on this plan are similar to that of corporate plans. Your contributions are restricted to the lower of 25 percent of earned income or $30,000.

QUALIFYING FOR KEOGHS

It is possible to set up and contribute to your plan without prior IRS approval. If you decide to do this, ask your local district director to review your plan. In setting up a trust, you will need to consult an attorney knowledgeable in the field to prepare the agreement and submit a request for IRS approval.

For a master or prototype plan, the sponsoring organization submits Form 4461 for a defined-contribution plan or Form 4461-A for a defined-benefit plan to the IRS. After approval, a number is assigned to the plan, then the sponsoring organization will advise you of the details of the plan.

8

ASSET ALLOCATION AND SOME BASIC TRUTHS ABOUT INVESTING

In planning for investment, there are some key things to keep in mind. Retirement planning is equivalent to life planning. Any strategy developed should not tie up your assets for long periods of time. Another thing you should do is read about and understand investment categories—how they operate in the long term and how they would impact on your status in relation to one another.

Also, as a wise retirement planner, you must be sure to diversify the plans and programs in which your money is placed. The financial market is volatile, and quite sensitive to world events. As an individual investor, you are much different from an institutional investor, whose actions influence the markets. Remember that the life of an individual far surpasses that of an institution.

As an individual, your investments should be measured in terms of your goals. That is to say, your main concern should be internal affairs as opposed to external forces. If you invest solely on the basis of market influences, more than likely you will run into some very serious difficulties.

ASSET ALLOCATION AND SOME BASIC TRUTHS ABOUT INVESTING

Also, with "sure-fire" long-shot opportunities, save yourself from later stress by only investing the minimum needed for a return once you have determined it is worth it.

Basically, you will be spreading your retirement monies over four categories: cash and cash equivalents, fixed income instruments, equities, and hard assets. A great deal of your return will depend on your choices among these categories. Obviously, with any investment, the more you hope to gain in returns, the more you will have to put down.

Say you've decided to take advantage of an opportunity to purchase a mutual fund that invests in fast-growing companies only. Let's also say that you've also decided to buy a long-term corporate bond so as not to put all your eggs in one basket.

Of course, dependent on the fluctuations of the market, you may do either very well or poorly. If inflation should rise, your mutual fund's value will also. On the other hand, a recession, lasting any period of time, may drive your shares down in value.

Your corporate bond, however, may be in a totally different state of affairs. An inflationary increase will lessen the value of your bond. A decrease in inflation will enhance the resale value and income value of the bond.

In that scenario, the losses in one area were compensated by gains in another area. That is the great value of diversifying.

MONTHLY AMOUNT NEEDED FOR RETIREMENT
For the Same Standard of Living You Will Need:

Annual Inflation Rate	Today, If You Can Get By On:	In 5 Years	In 10 Years	In 15 Years	In 20 Years	In 25 Years
6%	$ 1,000	$ 1,338	$ 1,791	$ 2,397	$ 3,207	$ 4,292
8%	1,000	1,469	2,159	3,172	4,661	6,848
10%	1,000	1,611	2,594	4,177	6,728	10,835
12%	1,000	1,762	3,106	5,474	9,646	17,000
14%	1,000	1,925	3,707	7,138	13,743	26,462

WHAT $100,000 WILL BE WORTH

Annual Inflation Rate	Today:	In 5 Years	In 10 Years	In 15 Years	In 20 Years	In 25 Years
6%	$ 100,000	$ 74,726	$ 55,839	$ 41,727	$ 31,180	$ 23,300
8%	100,000	68,058	46,319	31,524	21,455	14,602
10%	100,000	62,092	38,554	23,939	14,864	9,230
12%	100,000	56,743	32,197	18,270	10,367	5,882
14%	100,000	51,937	26,974	14,010	7,276	3,779

Source: Legg Mason Wood Walker, Inc.

9

MEDICARE AND YOU

Medicare is actually a two-part program that was developed in 1965. Part A provides coverage when you're hospitalized or in a skilled nursing home, and the second part, Part B, is for coverage of doctor bills and the expense of most other outpatient services.

Nearly all above the age of 65, and entitled to Social Security benefits, are eligible for Medicare. This includes the spouse of any eligible individual also. Those not entitled for whatever reason may enroll, but at an additional premium of $175 per month.

You should apply for the plan no later than three months before you reach the age of 65. Coverage will begin on then first day of the month you turn 65, regardless of whether you have retired or are still working.

Part A is automatically received by anyone that applies for Medicare. You have the option to enroll in Part B and will have to pay a monthly premium, which is usually deducted from your Social Security payments.

If you choose not to enroll in Part B immediately, you will run into extra costs when you do so. The late fee is 10 percent of the premium for each year you delay, and you

39

40   MEDICARE AND YOU

may only enroll in the months of January, February, or March. If you wait until retirement before enrolling, there may be up to one-year's delay before your coverage begins.

So take advantage of the plan. By doing so you will avoid frustrations later on down the line.

WHAT IS COVERED?

You should know that Part B of the coverage generally pays 80 percent of physicians' and surgeons' services, plus certain medical and health services. You are responsible for the remaining 20 percent. This applies in the case where you are seeing a practitioner whose fees are defined as "reasonable charges" by law. Request a list of health-care providers whose charges are in accordance with Medicare's guidelines.

In 1988, Congress expanded the amount of benefits provided under both parts of the coverage. Beginning in 1989, Medicare covers unlimited hospitalization charges after you pay the annual hospital deductible. In 1990, once you have made out-of-pocket expenses exceeding a "catastrophic" (as termed by the law) limit of $1,370 for covered medical expenses, Medicare will pay all "reasonable" charges thereafter.

To file your claims, all you need do for Part A services is sign the claim form to verify that you have received the stated services. The health-care provider then sends the claims to Medicare, which pays the hospital directly.

If your doctor is willing to accept your particular case, he or she will file the claim and is, again, paid directly by Medicare. If your doctor does not accept the assignment, you must fill out Form 1490S to receive your reimbursement from Medicare. Be sure to note on the claim that the reimbursement check is to come to you and not your doctor. The plan allows you 15 months to file a claim, dependent on the month your claim is incurred.

MEDIGAP

Medigap is a plan you can purchase from private insurance carriers. They've been designed to cover expenses not handled by Medicare. There are two different policies. The first handles only your share of costs covered by Medicare. The second, and the one most treasured by participants, pays surplus charges for your doctor bills and lab tests, and those that top Medicare's approved amounts. Note that the second policy is usually not more expensive than the first, but most likely you will be expected to have a very good health record.

MEDICAID

Medicaid is a program that was designed, originally, for those less economically advantaged. It serves to provide a kind of a safety net for retirees, provided they are in a particularly dire situation.

If your medical costs are exhausting nearly all of your income, and you have only $1,000 to $4,000 of your assets left, then you are a candidate to receive Medicaid. In the case that your spouse is in a nursing home, and the costs are being met by Medicare, you're allowed to receive no more than $1,500 a month in income.

Since the benefits you receive under Medicaid are dependent in part on the assets you personally hold, you may have to take extra measures to ensure that your heirs and offspring will also be comfortable. One way to do this is to transfer the titles of the assets you do have to family members other than your spouse. With the help of an attorney, you can thus create a Medicaid trust your offspring can rely on and you may continue to receive the benefits you need.

10

THE ESTIMATED TAX SYNDROME

As you know, the Federal government does expect income tax to be paid by every wage earner in the country. The method is not really an issue—you may estimate the amount owed for the upcoming year or do it through a payroll withholding arrangement offered by most companies. Taxes are due on the fifteenth of April each year.

The estimated tax method is most often used by self-employed persons, in which case payments are due on the 15th of January, April, June, and September. On each of these dates, you will have to pay estimated taxes to the Federal government—and perhaps to your state government as well.

The government doesn't care if you pay your taxes through payroll withholding or if you estimate your taxes throughout the year; just pay your taxes. If you choose to use the estimation method, you must keep the above-mentioned schedule in mind. If the due date happens to fall on a Saturday, Sunday, or legal holiday, you get a break. The postmark on the envelope is the date the IRS uses,

43

44   THE ESTIMATED TAX SYNDROME

provided your envelope is stamped by the U.S. Postal Service and not a private postage meter.

Suppose you don't make the quarterly payments or ante up enough at tax time? You will be penalized and you won't be able to deduct. You may be wondering what happens if you ask for an extension to file your 1040. Does that also mean you may cancel your first estimated tax payment? The answer is no, unfortunately. It doesn't matter whether you filed on time or requested an extension, your first estimated tax payment must still be paid on April 15.

The Federal government allows you to skip the January estimated tax payment on one condition: you file your return and pay your tax liability by January 31.

You may also skip quarterly payments if your estimated tax payment for the year, after deducting any taxes your employer withheld, is less than $500.

And please remember that your quarterly payments must equal either 100 percent of the tax you paid the previous year—that is, the amount shown on your last year's return—or 90 percent of the tax you'll owe in the current year. Suppose you underpay at tax time. You will be hit with an "underpayment penalty." The penalty is figured by the amount you fell short.

If you overpay on taxes, the Federal government gives you a choice. You can either apply the amount you overpaid to the taxes you'll owe next year, or collect a refund.

What if you retire, then take another salaried job? Or what if you're married and your spouse collects a regular paycheck? If you or your spouse don't withhold enough taxes from those paychecks, you'll have to pay the difference in the form of estimated tax payments.

TAX WORKSHEET

To keep track of what your tax deductions will amount to at the end of the year, use the worksheet below to list the expenses you can write off.

DEDUCTIONS

Mortgage Interest $ _____   IRA Contribution $ _____

Real Estate Taxes $ _____   Charitable
                                          Contributions $ _____

                                          Unreimbursed
State/Local Taxes $ _____   Business Expenses $ _____

                                          Alimony & Child
                                          Support Payments $ _____

Medical Expenses (over
3% of adjusted gross income)

                 $ _____

TOTAL DEDUCTIONS 1990 $ _____

The IRS provides many free booklets that can assist you in tax planning. Here is a partial listing of the publications and the areas they cover:

Publication 555: "Community Property and the Federal Income Tax"; Publication 448: "Estate & Gift Taxes"; Publication 590: "IRS Withdrawals"; Publication 544: "Sale and Disposition of Assets"; Publication 523: "Sale of Your Home"; Publication 505: "Tax Withholding and Estimated Tax"; Publication 519: "U.S. Tax Guide for Aliens";

46 THE ESTIMATED TAX SYNDROME

Publication 503: "Child and Dependent Care Credit for Household Employers."

For additional information and to order publications from the IRS, call 800-424-FORM. The IRS also has a 24-hour hotline with recorded announcements discussing more than 100 topics. Call 800-554-4477.

11

EARLY RETIREMENT POSSIBILITIES

Many companies provide early retirement plans that include anything from cash payments and an enhanced pension to post-retirement medical policies, and offers of outplacement counseling or job placement assistance. Other possible features are free medical and reduced life insurance coverage for one year.

In some cases, though, you may receive coverage until the age of 65, when Medicare takes over. Do your research into what your company offers.

In the case that your company wants to retire you early, you will be offered some kind of compensation. Options will vary dependent on the types of plans offered for the employees, and the amount of years you have already worked for the corporation. It is not unusual for a company to make an adjustment in your age, particularly if you are beyond the age of 55. If you are 59 and your company approaches you with an early retirement plan, they may calculate your benefits as though you are currently 62 or 63 years of age.

Doing so will make retirement more attractive to you

47

48   EARLY RETIREMENT POSSIBILITIES

at this point, because otherwise you'd receive less benefit payments due to your age.

Free medical and reduced rate group life insurance is another possible perk of choosing to retire early. Keep in mind that, with the rise of medical insurance costs, such offers are becoming increasingly scarce.

Some corporations might provide you with the option of participating in a plan to supplement Medicare. This allows you to enjoy the full coverage that would normally be available at normal retirement age.

SHOULD
I RETIRE
EARLY?

Most of us, who are employed by others, value the fact that we have steady income. So in considering early retirement, you should evaluate whether you can afford to. Get a pencil, note pad, calculator, and whatever else you may need to calculate what you will *not* be receiving once you stop working.

You should also be asking some very key questions. Will you have to take a cut in the pension benefits you would receive at normal retirement age? Will you receive adequate funds to cover your retirement until your Social Security begins? Also, be sure to compare the early retirement benefits you will receive to those you would receive, from your company, if you opted to keep working.

Critically speaking, you should assess the cash flow you will have available now and in the future. The method you choose to receive your benefits, be it by annuity or in a lump sum, should also be a factor to consider.

Finally, because you have retired from the company you've been with for many years, this does not mean your days of work are over. You may decide to pursue a totally different career—perhaps one that serves your artistic needs. That is where outplacement counselors may come into play. You also may find that your "after-career" will offer you benefits and/or compensation beyond your expectations.

Before making this major decision, be sure to consult a professional. You want to be sure that you weighed all possible considerations regarding this matter.

TEN MONEY TIPS FOR A PLEASANT JOINT RETIREMENT

One
Make joint financial decisions

Two
Save at least 10 percent of monthly income in a short-term emergency fund totaling between $2,000 and $5,000. One way is to do things that are pleasurable but don't cost money.

Three
Don't procrastinate about setting up financial goals.

Four
Properly insure your life, health, home, and auto. Review and perhaps replace any ordinary life policy which is more than five years old. It's probably obsolete.

Five
Maintain a good credit rating by paying your bills, not overspending and by avoiding most credit cards. Postpone buying expensive cars, lavish clothes, etc., during your early married years.

Six

Own rather than rent housing because of tax benefits.

Seven

For your child's college education, consider purchasing series EE U.S. savings bonds which allow you to defer tax on the interest until the child is 14. Also consider purchasing tax-exempt municipal bonds.

Eight

Postpone setting up an Individual Retirement Account until you are in your 40s. If you are self employed, though, you should seriously consider an IRA or a Keogh Plan.

Nine

For a long-range financial growth, invest in equities (mutual funds, stocks, bonds, limited partnership real estate, etc.), but purchase individual stocks only with the help of a professional money manager.

Ten

If your annual income is more than $50,000, you should consult a financial planner.

EARLY RETIREMENT POSSIBILITIES   51

Special
Section

Four Directories For Further Information On Retirement and Investment

---

(1) Money Management/Financial Planning

---

(2) Social Security

---

(3) Taxes

---

(4) Additional Organizations and Resources

MONEY MANAGEMENT

To write for brochures:

Fifteen Money Blunders
Public Relations Programs DA21
Corporate Communications
Aetna Life & Casualty
151 Farmington Avenue
Hartford, CT 06156
(203) 273-0123
Cost: Free

Managing Your Personal Finances: The Principles of Managing Your Finances (Part 1)
Consumer Information Center
PO Box 100
Pueblo, CO 81002
Cost: $3.25

How Much Are You Worth?
Federal Reserve Bank of Richmond
Public Services Department
PO Box 27622
Richmond, VA 23261
(804) 697-8000
Cost: Free

It's Your Money!
Order Processing Department
American Bankers Association
10 Jay Gould Court
Waldorf, MD 20601
(301) 663-5463
Cost: $2

Taking Charge of Your Money
AARP Fulfillment
1909 K Street, NW
Washington, D.C. 20049
(202) 872-4700
Cost: Free

Consumer Budget Planner
American Financial Services Association
1101 14th Street, NW
Washington, D.C. 20005
(202) 289-0400
Cost: Free

Consumers, Credit Bureaus and the Fair Credit Reporting Act
Member Services Department
Associated Credit Bureaus
PO Box 21830
Houston, TX 77218
(713) 492-8155
Cost: Free

54 EARLY RETIREMENT POSSIBILITIES

Equal Credit Opportunity and Age: Your Rights
Consumer Information Center-J
PO Box 100
Pueblo, CO 81002
Cost: Free

A Consumer Guide to Comprehensive Financial Planning
Registry of Financial Planning Practitioners
Two Concourse Parkway, Suite 800
Atlanta, GA 30328
(404) 395-1605
Cost: Free

Financial Management
Cornell Cooperative Extension
New York State College of Human Ecology
Cornell University
Ithaca, NY 14853-4401
(607) 255-7660 (several brochures available)
Cost: Under $1 each

Financial Side of Retirement Planning
National Resource Center for Consumers of Legal
  Services
124 D East Broad Street
Falls Church, VA 22046
(415) 622-6390
Cost: $.75

EARLY RETIREMENT POSSIBILITIES   55

Planning for Retirement Income
Bank of America National Trust and Savings Association
Box 37000
San Francisco, CA 94137
(415) 622-6390
Cost: $1

A Look at Retirement Planning After Tax Reform
Company Services
American Council of Life Insurance
1001 Pennsylvania Avenue, NW
Washington, DC 20004-2599
(202) 624-2000
Cost: Free

Books to purchase:

Complete Guide to Managing Your Money. Janet Bamford, Jeff Blyskal, Emily Card, and Aileen Jacobson. New York: Consumer Reports Books, 1988. $20.00.

Smart Money: How to Be Your Own Financial Adviser. Ken Dolan and Daria Dolan. New York: Random House, 1988. $19.95.

Retire in Style: The Lifetime Security Planning Guide. Edward Soltesz. Blue Ridge Summit, PA: Tab Books, 1988. $15.95.

What to Do With What You've Got: The Practical Guide to Money Management in Retirement. Peter Weaver and Annette Buchanan. Washington, D.C.: AARP Books, 1984. $7.95

EARLY RETIREMENT POSSIBILITIES

Organizations to contact:

American Financial Services Association, 1101 14th St., NW, Washington, DC 20005: Promotes the business of direct credit lending to consumers and conducts consumer education in money management principles and the uses of consumer credit. Publishes consumer budgeting guides.
(800) 843-3280;
(202) 289-0400.

Consumers Union of the United States, 256 Washington St., Mount Vernon, NY 10553: An information and counseling service that helps individuals overcome problems with family income expenditures. Distributes a magazine.
(914) 667-9400.

SOCIAL SECURITY

To write for brochures:

Estimating Your Social Security Retirement Check
Social Security Administration
Public Information
Security Boulevard
Baltimore, MD 21235
(301) 965-3970
Cost: Free

How Work Affects Your Social Security Check
Social Security Administration
Public Information
Security Boulevard
Baltimore, MD 21235
(301) 965-3970
Cost: Free

Retirement? Remember Social Security
Social Security Administration
Public Information
Security Boulevard
Baltimore, MD 21235
(301) 965-3970
Cost: Free

Social Security and Your Right to Representation
Social Security Administration
Public Information
Security Boulevard
Baltimore, MD 21235
(301) 965-3970
Cost: Free

Social Security: Crises, Questions, Remedies
Public Affairs Pamphlets
381 Park Avenue South
New York, NY 10016
(212) 683-4331
Cost: $1

Books to purchase:

The Complete and Easy Guide to Social Security and Medicare. Sixth Revised Edition, Madison, CT: Fraser, 1989. $6.95.

No Nonsense Guide Understanding Social Security. Gerald Gladney. Stamford, CT: Longmeadow Press, 1991. $4.50.

Your Guide to Social Security Benefits, 1989-90. Leona G. Rubin. New York: Facts on File: 1989. $9.95.

TAXES

To write for brochures:

18 Ways to Save Money on Income Taxes
Dean Witter Reynolds
Chevy Chase Brunch
2 Wisconsin Circle, Suite 330
(800) 443-4503
Cost: Free

People Helping People
AARP Fulfillment
1909 K Street, NW
Washington, DC 20049
(202) 872-4700
Cost: Free

Tax-Aide Brochure
AARP Fulfillment
1909 K Street, NW
Washington, DC 20049
(202) 872-4700
Cost: Free

Books to purchase:

Guide to Income Tax Preparation: 1989 Edition.
Warren Esnau. New York: Consumer Reports Books,
1988. $9.95.
**The Personal Tax Advisor: Understanding the New
Tax Law.** Cliff Robertson. Blue Ridge Summit, PA: TAB
Books, 1987. $12.95

ADDITIONAL RESOURCES AND ORGANIZATIONS

Here is a listing of state aging commission offices. These offices can be of great assistance to you.

Alabama

Commission on Aging, 502 Washington Avenue, Montgomery, AL 36130.

Alaska

Older Alaskans Commission, PO Box C, Mail Station 0209, Juneau, AK 99811.

American Samoa

Territorial Administration on Aging, Government of American Samoa, Pago Pago, American Samoa 96799.

Arizona

Aging and Adult Administration, 1400 West Washington Street, Phoenix, AZ 85007.

Arkansas

Office of Aging and Adult Services, Department of Human Services, PO Box 1473, Little Rock, AR 72203.

California

Department of Aging, 1600 K Street, Sacramento, CA 95814.

EARLY RETIREMENT POSSIBILITIES   61

Colorado
Aging and Adult Services Division, Department of Social Services, 717 17th Street, 11th Floor, Denver, CO 80218.

Connecticut
Department of Aging, 174 Main Street, Hartford, CT 06106.

Delaware
Department of Health and Social Services, Division of Aging, 1901 North DuPont Hwy., New Castle, DE 19720.

District of Columbia
DC Office on Aging, 1424 K Street, NW, 2nd Floor, Washington, DC 20005.

Florida
Aging and Adult Services, 1321 Winewood Blvd., Room 323, Tallahassee, FL 32301.

Georgia
Office of Aging, 878 Peachtree St., NE, Room 632, Atlanta, GA 30309.

Guam
Office of Aging, Government of Guam, PO Box 2816, Agana, Guam 96910.

Hawaii
Executive Office on Aging, 335 Merchant St., Room 241, Honolulu, HI 96813.

Idaho

Idaho Office on Aging, Statehouse, Room 114, Boise, ID 83720.

Illinois

Department on Aging, 421 E. Capitol Ave., Springfield, IL 62701.

Indiana

Aging Division, Department of Human Services, PO Box 7083, Indianapolis, IN 46204.

Iowa

Department of Elder Affairs, 914 Grand Ave., Ste. 236, Des Moines, IA 50319.

Kansas

Department on Aging, 610 W. 10th St., Topeka, KS 66612.

Kentucky

Division for Aging Services, Department for Social Services, DHR Building, 275 E. Main St., 6th floor West, Frankfurt, KY 40621.

Louisiana

Governor's Office of Elder Affairs, PO Box 80374, Baton Rouge, LA 70898.

Maine

Bureau of Maine's Elderly, Statehouse, Station 11, Augusta, ME 04333.

Maryland

Office on Aging, 301 West Preston Street, 10th Floor, Baltimore, MD 21201.

Massachusetts

Executive Office of Elder Affairs, 38 Chauncey Street, Boston, MA 02111.

Michigan

Office of Services to the Aging, PO Box 30026, Lansing, MI 48909.

Minnesota

Minnesota Board on Aging, 7th and Robert Streets, St. Paul, MN 55101.

Mississippi

Council on Aging, 301 West Pearl Street, Jackson, MI 39201.

Missouri

Division on Aging, PO Box 1337, Jefferson City, MO 65102.

Montana

Aging Services Bureau, Department of Family Services, PO Box 8005, Helena, MT 59604.

Nebraska

Nebraska Department on Aging, State House Station 95044, Lincoln, NE 68509.

Nevada

Division for Aging Services, Department of Human Resources, 505 East King Street, Room 101, Carson City, NV 89710.

New Hampshire

Division of Elderly and Adult Services, 6 Hazen Drive, Concord, NH 03301.

New Jersey

Division on Aging, Department of Community Affairs, 363 State Street, CN 807, Trenton, NJ 08625.

New Mexico

State Agency on Aging, 224 East Palace Avenue, Fourth Floor, Santa Fe, NM 87501.

New York

New York State Office for the Aging, Agency Building Two, Empire State Plaza, Albany, NY 12223.

North Carolina

Division on Aging, Department of Human Resources, 1985 Umstead Drive, Raleigh, NC 27603.

North Dakota

Aging Services, Department of Human Services, State Capitol Building, Bismarck, ND 58505.

Ohio

Ohio Department of Aging, 50 West Broad Street, 9th Floor, Columbus, OH 43215.

Oklahoma

Special Unit on
Aging, PO Box
25352, Oklahoma
City, OK 73215.

Oregon

Senior Services
Division, State of
Oregon, Department
of Human Resources,
313 Public Service
Building, Salem, OR
97310.

Pennsylvania

Department of
Aging, 231 State
Street, Harrisburg,
PA 17101.

Puerto Rico

Gericulture
Commission,
Department of Social
Services, PO Box
11398, Santurce,
Puerto Rico 00910.

Rhode Island

Department of
Elderly Affairs, 79
Washington Street,
Providence, RI
02903.

South Carolina

Commission on
Aging, 915 Main
Street, Columbia, SC
29201.

South Dakota

Office of Adult
Services and Aging,
700 Governors Drive,
Pierre, SD 57501.

Tennessee

Commission on
Aging, 706 Church
Street, Nashville,
TN 37219.

Texas

Texas Department
on Aging, PO Box
12786, Capitol
Station, Austin, TX
78711.

Utah

Division on Aging and Adult Services, PO Box 45500, Salt Lake City, UT 84115.

Vermont

Office on Aging, 103 S. Main Street, Waterbury, VT 05676.

Virginia

Department for the Aging, 101 North 14th Street, 18th Floor, Richmond, VA 23219.

Virgin Islands

Commission on Aging, 6F Habensights Mall, Charlotte Amalie, St. Thomas, Virgin Islands 00807.

Washington

Aging and Adult Services Administration, OB-44A, Olympia, WA 98504.

West Virginia

Commission on Aging, State Capitol, Charleston, WV 25305.

Wisconsin

Bureau on Aging, PO Box 7851, Madison, WI 53707.

Wyoming

Commission on Aging, Hathaway Building, Room 139, WY 82002.

GLOSSARY

ANNUITY: Contract sold by insurance companies that pays a monthly, quarterly, semiannual, or annual income benefit for the life of the person or annuitant. The annuitant can never outlive the income from the annuity.

AVERAGED INDEXED MONTHLY EARNINGS (AIME): A calculated set of figures that is used to arrive at a worker's Primary Insurance Amount (PIA) for Social Security benefits.

BENEFICIARY: Designation by the policyholder of a life insurance policy indicating to whom the proceeds are to be paid upon the insured's death or when an endowment matures.

BENEFIT: Monetary or in kind sum paid or payable to a recipient for which the insurance company has received the premiums.

CALENDAR QUARTER: A three-month period that is applied to the Social Security eligibility of the individual.

CHARTERED FINANCIAL PLANNER or CONSULTANT (ChFC): A professional designation awarded by the American College or its designate. In addition to professional business experience in financial planning, recipients are required to pass national examinations in insurance, investments, taxation, employee benefit plans, estate planning, accounting,

67

68   GLOSSARY

and management. ChFC holders are proficient in personal financial planning.

CHARTERED LIFE UNDERWRITER (GLU): Professional designation also conferred by the American College similar to ChFC with additional requirements for knowledge of economics. A holder of CLU certificate is technically proficient to help plan individual life insurance programs.

CLAIM: Request by a policyholder for indemnification by an insurance company for loss incurred from an insured peril.

COST OF LIVING ADJUSTMENT (COLA): Automatic adjustment applied to Social Security retirement payments when the consumer price index increases at a rate of at least 3%, the first quarter of one year to the first quarter of the next year.

CURRENTLY INSURED: An insured status for a person who has not earned fully insured status. One is currently insured if one has acquired at least six quarters of coverage during the full 13 quarter period prior to a petition for Social Security benefits.

DEDUCTIBLE: Amount of loss that insured pays in a claim; including: 1) Absolute dollar amount—Amount the insured must pay before company will pay, up to the limits of the policy; and 2) Time period amount—Length of time the insured must wait before any benefit payments are made by the insurance company. It is usually applicable to disability policies. Deductible also refers to the amount of tax-deferrable income an individual can contribute to a qualified retirement plan.

DEFINED BENEFIT PLAN: Retirement plan under which benefits are fixed in advance by formula.

DEFINED CONTRIBUTION PLAN: A retirement plan under which contributions are fixed in advance by formula, and benefits vary. These plans are frequently used by organizations that must know what cost employee benefits will be in the years ahead.

DISABILITY: The inability to engage in any substantial

GLOSSARY 69

gainful activity by reason of any medically determined physical or mental impairment which can be expected to last for a continuous period of not less than 12 months.

EMPLOYEE STOCK OWNERSHIP PLAN (ESOP): Type of benefit in which an employee obtains shares of stock in the company, the amount normally determined by the employee's level of compensation. ESOPs usually act as a leverage tool through which the business is able to obtain a source of capital.

ENDOWMENT INSURANCE: A life insurance policy where a policyholder receives the face value of a policy if the insured survives the endowment period. If the policyholder does not survive, a beneficiary receives the face value of the policy.

FEDERAL DEPOSIT INSURANCE CORPORATION (FDIC): An agency formed as a result of bank failures in the 1930s. It is designed to insure the deposits of customers of member banks.

FEDERAL INSURANCE CONTRIBUTIONS ACT (FICA): The Social Security tax that is deposited into the Social Security trust fund out of which benefits are paid.

FILING: Filing a claim is key to receiving any Social Security benefits. No benefit is automatically allocated no matter the eligibility.

401(k) PLAN: An employer-sponsored retirement savings program named for the section of the Internal Revenue Code that permits it. This plan allows employees to invest pre-tax dollars that are often matched in some portion by the employer.

403(b) PLAN: A retirement plan offered by public employers and tax-exempt organizations. Under the plan, certain tax-exempt organizations such as public school systems can make payments for retirement annuity policies for their employees and have payments excluded from the employee's gross income for tax purposes.

FULLY INSURED: A fully insured person under Social Security is generally a per-

70 GLOSSARY

son who has earned 40 quarters of coverage. See Currently Insured.

HIDDEN INSURANCE: Insurances attached to standard purchases that increase the cost of the purchase. Hidden insurances include extended warranties, auto service contracts, credit life and disability and mortgage life insurance.

INDEMNITY: Guaranteed compensation for an insured loss.

INDIVIDUAL RETIREMENT ACCOUNT (IRA);, A fund first established under the Tax Reform Act of 1986 where an individual employee can contribute up to $2,000 per year. Income levels and eligibility for an employee pension plan determines whether or not the employee's contribution or a percentage of it is tax deductible.

JOINT AND SURVIVOR ANNUITY (J&S): An annuity that continues income payments as long as one annuitant, out of two or more annuitants, remains alive.

KEOGH PLAN: An individual retirement program estab-

lished by Congress in 1962 for self-employed individuals. The individual can make non-deductible voluntary contributions and tax-deductible contributions subject to certain maximum limits. It gets its name from its sponsor, New York Representative Eugene Keogh.

LUMP-SUM DEATH PAYMENT: A small one time payment for the eligible survivor of a fully or currently insured individual of the Social Security program.

LICENSED INSURANCE ADVISOR (LIA): Licensed granting legal authority to conduct insurance business in a particular state. In many states, agents and brokers must pass a written exam as a prerequisite to being licensed. The license is usually issued for one or two year periods, and then must be renewed.

MEDICAID: A needs-based medical assistance program financed jointly by Federal and state governments, for the aged, blind, disabled and families with dependent children.

MEDICAID TRUST: An arrangement where an individ-

GLOSSARY 71

ual arranges to have the title to their assets transferred to a designated individual — usually offspring — in order to insure that the individual is eligible for Medicaid benefits.

MEDICARE: A health insurance program paid for in part by specified income tax deductions. Medicare is organized in two parts. Part A covers hospitalization costs. Part B is a voluntary component that covers physician services.

MEDIGAP: Medical supplement insurance sold by private insurers to cover the coinsurance of deductible health costs not covered by Medicare.

OLD AGE, SURVIVORS, AND DISABILITY INSURANCE (OASDI): Federal social insurance program that provides monthly benefits to qualified retirees, their dependents, their survivors, and in some cases, disabled workers.

PENSION PLAN: Retirement program to provide employees and sometimes spouses, with a monthly income payment for the rest of their lives. To qualify, an employee must have met minimum age and service requirements. See also Defined Benefit Plan and Defined Contribution Plan.

POLICY: Contract or written agreement which puts insurance coverage into effect.

PORTFOLIO: The total package of policies underwritten by any given insurance company.

POST RETIREMENT FUNDING: A method of funding a medical and/or pension plan after a worker retires. An employer purchases an annuity or sets aside a sum when an employee retires that will pay a specified benefit for the lifetime of the retiree.

PREMIUM: Rate the insured is charged by the insured for his or her expected loss or risk.

PRIMARY INSURANCE AMOUNT (PIA): Monthly benefit payable to retired or disabled workers under Social Security. It is calculated by using the average monthly earnings of the covered person while working. Benefits for spouse, other dependents, and survivors are fig-

GLOSSARY

ured as a percentage of the PIA. A worker who takes early retirement may receive a portion of the PIA at age 62. The PIA is used to calculate most other benefits.

PROFIT SHARING PLAN: An arrangement by an employer in which employees share in the profits of the business. To be qualified for tax benefits, the plan must use a predetermined formual for contributions and for distribution of benefits to participatants upon attainment of a specified age, or in case of illness, disability, retirement or death.

QUALIFIED PLAN: Term applied to pension and retirement programs that are eligible for a special tax deferred status.

RETIREMENT AGE: Currently stands at 65 in Social Security parlance. By 2027 it will be 67. The retirement age is the age at which a fully or currently insured claimant can receive the full retirement benefits for which they are eligible.

SELF-EMPLOYED INDIVIDUAL RETIREMENT ACT: See KEOGH Plan.

SELF-INSURANCE: Protecting against loss by setting aside one's own money.

SINGLE-LIFE ANNUITY: An annuity that continues income payments as long as the annuitant lives.

SOCIAL INSURANCE: A mandatory employee benefit plan under which participants are entitled to a series of benefits as a matter of right. The plan is administered by a Federal or state government agency and is designed to provide a minimum standard of living for those in lower and middle income groups. See also Social Security.

SOCIAL SECURITY: A series of government-sponsored social insurance programs that include retirement benefits, disability benefits, public assistance, workmen's compensation, food stamps, Medicare, and Medicaid.

SOCIAL SECURITY ACT: Congressional act that established a variety of programs under two general headings—social insurance and public assistance that provides for needs of individuals and families.

INDEX

AGI (Adjusted Gross Income), 20
Annuities, 16
Books to Purchase, 55
CD (Certificates of Deposit), 21, 29-30
Deductibles, 20
Disability Benefits, 5
Divorced Spouse, 7
Early Retirement, 48
EE U.S. Savings Bonds, 50
ESOPs (Employee Stock Ownership Plans), 15
FDIC (Federal Deposit Insurance Corporation), 2, 28
FICA (Federal Insurance Contributions Act), 10
Form 1490s, 40
Form 4461, 33
Fully Insured, 6
Fund Transfers, 20
Glossary, 67
IRAs (Individual Retirement Accounts), 2, 11, 17, 19, 23
IRS (Internal Revenue Service), 13, 33, 46
Joint Retirement Plan, 49
J&S (Joint and Survivor) Annuities, 16-17
Keogh, Eugene, 2

KOEGHS, 2, 31
Lump-Sum Withdrawals, 16
Medicaid, 41
Medicare, 6, 39, 47
Medigap, 41
Money Management, 52
Money Market Plans, 27
Municipal Bonds, 21
Mutual Funds, 21, 27, 36
NCUA (National Credit Union Administration), 28
Organizations to Contact, 56
Pension Plans, 14
Profit-Sharing Plan, 15
Puerto Rico, 11
Qualified Plans, 13
Retirement Benefits, 5
Roll-Over, 21
Self-Employed Individuals Retirement Act, 2
Social Security, 8, 39, 57
Social Security Act, 5
Social Security Administration, 1, 6-8, 10
Survivor's Benefits, 5
Taxes, 59
Tax Worksheet, 45
Underpayment Penalty, 44

IRENE BLANKSON is a journalist who graduated from New York University. She has written for many professional publications and has done extensive work in the banking industry.

KEVIN POWELL is a veteran journalist who has written on the subjects of economics and finance for major publications.